Dialogue Exchange
Interactive English Listening and Speaking for Beginners

D. L. Bradbury

Planet B Publishing
Vancouver, BC
Canada

Reference/Teaching English as a Second Language/Listening and Speaking

Copyright (c) 2013 D L Bradbury.

All rights reserved. Photocopying permitted for ESL classroom use. Photocopying of short selections permitted for teacher training purposes. Any other use of any part of this publication reproduced or transmitted in any form or by any means, electronic, mechanical, email, photocopying, recording, or otherwise, without the prior written consent of the publisher is an infringement of copyright law. Any commercial or noncommercial redistribution or reproduction of all or part of this publication is strictly prohibited under international law. The recipient of downloads does not have the right to give, lend, or sell them without express permission of the publisher. Derivative translations also subject to copyright.

Canadian Cataloguing in Publication Data

Bradbury, D L 1959 –
    Dialogue Exchange: Interactive English Listening and Speaking for Beginners
    D L Bradbury. – Ist ed.

ISBN 978-1-4910-3605-1

Catalogue data available from Library and Archives Canada

Planet B Publishing
214A - 2416 Main Street
Vancouver, BC
Canada
V5T 3E2

www.dialogueexchange.com

Dedication

This book is for my students.

Acknowledgments

I would like to express my thanks to the instructors and staff at the University of British Columbia, Vancouver Community College, Pacific Immigrant Resources Society, and Immigrant Services Society of British Columbia. I'd like to thank Janet Massaro, Marni Segal, Diane Millar, and especially Robert Ives and Grant Lovelock for sharing teaching strategies. I'd like to acknowledge Judy Gilbert, Lillian Butovsky, and Esther Podoliak whose work informed my own. Many thanks also to Pat Steiner, Sandra Price-Hosie, Christine Parkin, Vanny Seak, and Peter Quartermain for assistance and inspiration. Much gratitude also goes to Jennifer Pearson Terrell, Mindy Zhou, Sarah Dean, Virginia Armitage, and Mark Hill for their help and support with this project.

Preface

Have you ever studied a language in an academic setting, only to find that you can't use what you have learned? It may be easy to remember some vocabulary or to pass exams in your target language, but can you hold a conversation in it, or even follow one? It is difficult to retain a new language without actively using it.

Dialogue Exchange aims to address this problem. It provides beginners with not only the tools, but also with the practice required to have authentic conversations in their target language.

Dialogue Exchange is a theme-based, student-centred, interactive listening and speaking program that incorporates reading, writing, pronunciation, vocabulary, and correction. It is intended as part of a larger curriculum that includes grammar. *Dialogue Exchange* uses everyday themes and language, and is designed for communicative competence. Activities begin with controlled practice and gradually progress toward freer practice.

Instructions include teaching techniques and classroom management strategies that will allow even novice instructors to use the materials effectively. Each dialogue can be used as a starting point for generating new language.

This teaching manual is ideal for immersion environments where the teacher does not speak the language(s) of the students. This material is written for adult learners, and can be used in beginner classes from all backgrounds. While there is definitely some overlap when teaching K-12, adaptation may be necessary. For example, younger students may not require as much help with pronunciation.

Dialogue Exchange is designed to teach beginners in a classroom setting how to speak English; however, because lessons are based on visuals, it can be adapted to teach any language. The materials can be used by the instructor to learn some of the students' language(s). As well, most of the activities can be adapted for one-on-one tutoring or for language exchanges.

Contents

Part One—For the Instructor

1. How to Use this Book..3

2. Presenting a Dialogue...4

3. Putting Students in Groups...7

4. Review Activities for Single Dialogues..8

5. Extension Activities for Single Dialogues..12

6. Review Activities for Vocabulary...14

7. Review Activities for Multiple Dialogues...16

8. Correction...19

9. Appendix A: Teaching the Basics..145

10. Appendix B: Reference Material for Pronunciation...151

11. Frequently Asked Questions..154

12. Grids..156

Contents

Part Two—For the Students

1. Giving Personal Information..23

2. Asking for Help with English...31

3. Ordering a Meal...39

4. Shopping..47

5. Calling for Help in an Emergency..55

6. Asking for Directions...63

7. Renting an Apartment...71

8. Taking the Bus...79

9. Making Appointments...87

10. Opening a Bank Account...95

11. Applying for a Job..103

12. Joining a Community Centre...111

13. Checking in at the Airport...119

14. Renting a Hotel Room...127

15. Taking a Taxi..135

Instructions for Teachers

How to Use This Book

Presentation and Review Activities should be divided up over several days, for a total of three to five sessions for teaching and reviewing each dialogue, depending on the level of your class. Add three to five more days for the Extension Activities and Vocabulary Review. Allow about an hour for the material each day. *There are dozens of exercises and variations, but it is not necessary or advisable to do all of them, especially for higher (more proficient) classes.* Choose the ones that are best-suited to your class, or vary the activities with each chapter taught. Ensure that students do lots of pair or group work, because these activities will give them more speaking practice. Items needed for each exercise are set out in **bold**.

Some chapters require that students first understand some basic vocabulary, such as names of countries, food, numbers, parts of the body, dates, and time. Suggestions for teaching this material can be found in Appendix A on page 145.

If you feel that the content of a particular chapter does not meet the needs of your students, omit it. Feel free to change the order in which chapters are taught if this would be more appropriate for your class. Once you have taught three chapters, review them together as a set. Do this periodically to ensure that students retain what they have learned.

The picture cards and dialogue strips work best if photocopied on brightly-coloured card stock or at least on coloured paper. Card stock is worth the investment, because everything will look more appealing and course materials will last longer.

In order to make presentations more interactive, always elicit as much material as possible from students. Break down the steps for students, and ask yes or no questions if necessary. Students will remember rules better if they have had to work them out for themselves first. As well, some students may know some of the vocabulary already, because they have been exposed to English previously or because they are studying at home. Eliciting material rewards students for their knowledge and for thinking independently. Only provide material as a last resort if you are getting blank stares or incorrect responses.

Presenting a Dialogue*

Photocopy a dialogue onto card stock, and cut out the nine pictures. You may find it helpful to pre-teach some key vocabulary words. Gather your students around a table, and put the pictures in order. Have students look at all of the pictures, then at each picture. *Elicit as much of the dialogue as possible from the students.* You will have to provide some of it.

Point at each picture, and have the students repeat each line after you. Do this until the students can produce each line of dialogue as a group while you silently point at each picture. Next, call on individuals at random to repeat lines after you. Give easier lines to less proficient students.

Have the students return to their desks, and give them **photocopies of the dialogue pictures**. Divide the board into nine squares. Elicit the dialogue from the students, and write their answers on the board. Using a different colour of ink for each speaker in the dialogue will make things more clear for the students.

Have the students copy the dialogue from the board into the space beneath the pictures on their copies. It is best not to let the students copy until you have finished speaking; if they copy while you are talking, the activity will lose focus, because it is too difficult for beginning students to contribute to class and write at the same time. Copying after you have finished gives the class quiet time to digest new information, and it facilitates memory.

Be sure to address any issues, cultural or otherwise, that may arise. Is it okay to ask people if they're married? Is it okay to ask a stranger for help in a coffee shop? Does it matter if the person is of the opposite sex? What number do you call for emergency services? What are the symptoms of a heart attack? Does the woman on the bus really want to see the driver later?

Note: If students suggest correct lines of dialogue that differ from what I have used, you may want to use what they have chosen. You will have to do some typing in that case, and a blank grid is provided on page 156.

If your class already knows more than 30 per cent of the content of the dialogue and their responses are correct, but differ from the language that I have chosen, it is more appropriate to make use of their responses during the presentation, and to type these responses into the blank grid for review work. Subsequent worksheets should also be adapted or omitted, and the class should move on fairly quickly to the Extension Activities section.

For lower classes, alternative language can be introduced during the review process. Lower students will benefit from some initial language modeling, and they will ultimately perform better during the more-demanding, freer-practice Extension Activities because of this practice.

Dialogue Exchange 4

Choral Repetition*

Choral repetition allows students to practice pronunciation in a non-threatening atmosphere and to memorize common sentence patterns rather than become confused by the sometimes complicated grammar behind them. Because everyone is speaking, choral repetition is a good use of valuable class time. Calling on individual students takes longer, especially if you have a large class, and it can be intimidating for students who are speaking and boring for those who are not. It's best to limit the use of this latter method and to check individual pronunciation while students are working in pairs.

Mark the dialogue on the board for sentence stress, intonation, linking, and reductions. For example:

Have the students copy the marked dialogue into their notebooks. (Rhythm will vary according to the dialect you speak. For reference material on rhythm, see Appendix B on page 151.)

Read the dialogue line by line, and have the students repeat after you. The backward buildup method works best for longer lines of dialogue and for questions. Have the students repeat after you:

> apartment?
> an apartment?
> or an apartment?
> house or an apartment?
> a house or an apartment?
> that a house or an apartment?
> Is that a house or an apartment?

(Don't write the line on the board as it appears immediately above; just point to the words as you say them and have students repeat.) Illustrate intonation by using your left hand the way a conductor would, and show sentence stress by stamping one foot. Have students do this also.

Do the repetitions chorally. Repeat each step as many times as necessary. Finally, call on individual students at random, giving easier lines to lower students.

This is a good time to spend a couple of minutes dealing with any pronunciation problems, but don't let them derail your lesson. Serious pronunciation issues should be addressed later in a dedicated lesson.

Once the students are reasonably proficient at repeating the dialogue after you, divide the class in two and have one side of the class read to the other side. When they have finished, have the two sides switch roles.

Practicing a Dialogue in Pairs

Have each student practice the dialogue with the person sitting next to him or her (not in front of the class). Let them read from their books or from the board. Circulate and answer questions. Make sure students switch roles. When the students have practiced enough, match them with new partners who are sitting as far away as possible from each other. Have the new partners call the dialogue to each other from across the class, one pair at a time. (The teacher should always move as far away as possible from students who are speaking in front of the class, in order to get them to project their voices. Nominating students at random will help them stay focused on the activity.)

When a student makes a pronunciation error while speaking in front of the class, say the word correctly, have the individual repeat it, then say "everyone" and have the class repeat it. Do this a couple of times if necessary. This method will reinforce the idea that the whole class could use practice, and it should make the individual less self-conscious.

In order to maintain focus, it's best to do half of the pairs before a break, especially if you have a large class. Finish when you return.

Presentation, choral repetition, and pair practice can be split up over two sessions.

Putting Students in Groups

There are several ways to group students. *What is critical for the success of your class is that students work with several different partners each day. Ultimately, each student should work with every other member of the class.* This method will make your students more comfortable with each other and with the new language. It will also make the class more social and more fun, and it should help with attendance. Students will make more friends, and if they speak different languages, they will use English to communicate with each other outside of class. Using the language in everyday situations like this is the best way to improve speaking skills, and it's more fun than studying.

Coloured Strip Method

Cut up some **strips of coloured paper**. The number of colours you use will equal the number of students in each group. If you have a lower, less proficient class, put up to four students in each group. If you have a higher class, put fewer students in each group. Ensure that you have enough strips for all of the students and an equal number of each colour. As you walk around the class, first hand out all of the green strips of paper, then all of the red strips, and so on. Give friends the same colour of strip. When you are finished, have the students form groups that have one student with each colour—this way, friends will not end up in the same group, and cliques will be less likely to form.

At times, you may want to have one higher, more proficient student in each group. To do this, give the higher students strips of the same colour.

Numbering Method

This is a faster way to do the same thing, but it allows for less manipulation. If you want to divide the class into two teams, move from one side of the room to the other, pointing at students who are sitting next to each other. Say, "I will give you a number. Remember your number. One, two. One, two. One, two….Team one here, team two over there." If you want four teams, use the same method, but count to four instead of two.

It may not be necessary to go through all of these steps every time you group the students. Once the students understand what you want, you can simply say, "Work with someone new (for today)."

Review Activities for Single Dialogues

Activities are in approximate order of difficulty, with the easier ones first. It's not necessary to do every exercise; choose the ones that best suit your class. These activities should not be done on the same day that the dialogue is introduced.

Chop and Scramble*

Make sure you have **a pair of scissors** on hand. Photocopy the words for the dialogue (the second page in each chapter) onto card stock, and cut them into strips, so that each line of dialogue is on a separate strip. Photocopy the pictures onto card stock and cut out each panel. Make **a set of dialogue strips and cut up pictures for each group of two to four students** in your class. Use smaller groups for higher classes. Photocopying each set on a different colour of paper will help to keep the dialogues straight later.

Put the students in groups (page 7), and have them match the lines of dialogue to the pictures. Monitor the groups. If they make mistakes, move any incorrect lines to the bottom, and have them try again. When they have completed the activity successfully, have each group read the dialogue aloud (to you, not to the whole class). Assist with pronunciation. When they are finished, smile, scramble up the strips, say "again," and then move to the next table.

Once students are proficient at the above activity, cut each strip of dialogue in half and scramble up all of the strips. Have the students reassemble the dialogue and read it again. Continue with this process until each word is a single piece and the students can put all of the pieces together like a puzzle. (For lower groups in a multilevel class, don't cut the pieces down to single words. This will allow them to complete the activity in the same time as their peers.) Alternatively, you may want to group lower-level students with higher ones and let them help each other. Students should read the dialogue aloud several times during this activity.

This activity should help students when it comes to unstressed words, such as "is" and "the." They may have difficulty hearing these sounds, and consequently, difficulty reproducing them. Save picture pieces and words for later review.

Listening Exercise for Rhythm*

Rhythm can vary according to dialect. For reference material on rhythm, see Appendix B on page 151. **Worksheets** are provided in each chapter. Give each student a worksheet and have them listen while you read the dialogue. **It's best to record your voice**, so it is the same every time, and to have another teacher read the other role. Pause after each line.

Have students mark the dialogue for sentence stress, intonation, linking, and reductions. *This will be too much all at once for beginning students, so start with sentence stress and introduce the other items gradually as students are ready for them. For some classes, sentence stress alone may be enough.* **Make sure you change the instructions on the students' worksheets to reflect what you are asking them to do.**

To teach sentence stress, play the recording and tell students to circle the loudest, strongest word in each sentence. (Sometimes there will be two words.) Monitor the students to make sure they are completing the task successfully. Play the tape as many times as necessary.

Dialogues are a good way to teach sentence stress, because the focus of each line changes as new information is provided. When they have finished the worksheet, elicit the answers from the students. Ask students:

> Which word is the loudest and strongest?
> Which word has new information?
> Which word is the most important in the sentence?
> Is it a noun, a verb, an adjective or something else?

After the whole exercise has been corrected, elicit the rules. For example, sentence stress is the highest level of stress and normally falls on one or sometimes two words in the sentence that contain new information. Usually these will be content words: nouns, main verbs, adjectives, adverbs, question words, and negative contractions. Ask students:

> Which words are strongest? Why? (Words with new information are strongest.)
> What part of speech are they usually? Nouns? Verbs? Anything else? Why? (These parts of speech usually contain the new information.)
> Which words are weaker or more quiet? (The words with less information are weaker.)

You may have to provide some of the answers, but always give the class a chance first. Ask yes or no questions if necessary. After a couple of chapters—and only if it is appropriate for your class—ask students to mark intonation, then linking, and finally reductions.

The point of this activity is to have students listen and read at the same time, and to pay attention to the whole line, rather than focusing on a blank. These exercises connect written and spoken language, and address common speaking errors like staccato speech and missing function words. Focusing on sentence stress helps students listen for gist. Students who master English rhythm are easier to understand, so they will have longer conversations with native speakers, and thus will get more practice and improve more quickly than those who don't. Making the recording available to students for homework will allow them to practice proper rhythm in a relaxed atmosphere, instead of practicing pronunciation errors. As you record, allow enough space after each line for students to be able to repeat after you.

Variation: For higher classes, use the listening worksheet to make a pair dictation. Make two copies and label them A and B. Mark the rhythm for speaker A on the **A worksheet**. Mark the rhythm for speaker B on the **B worksheet**. Give out the A sheets on one side of the class and the B sheets on the other. Let students choose, but ask them to work with partners that they haven't worked with yet that day. The A students read the text while the B students mark the rhythm on their worksheets. They switch roles, and then compare their papers when they are finished. Monitor pairs, and then elicit the rules when students have completed the activity.

For variety, other source materials, such as songs or short stories, can also be used to teach rhythm.

Teacher-to-Student Dictation*

Photocopy about five random lines of dialogue onto card stock and cut them into strips. If you have, for example, 20 students in your class, use five lines of dialogue and make four copies of each line. Make sure you have one strip for each student.

If they need it, let students study for a couple of minutes, and then have them open their notebooks to a fresh page. Dictate the lines of dialogue to the students. Write difficult words on the board and tell students not to worry too much about spelling. Speak at about 50 per cent of normal speed, with normal stress, intonation, linking, and reductions. Repeat the lines as many times as necessary (at least four or five times). Write, "Can you repeat that, please?" on the board, and have students ask you the question as needed. Walk around the class and make sure the students are able to write down what you are saying. If they are having difficulty, ask them how many words are in the line of dictation, then use your fingers to count off the words as you repeat each line.

When you have finished the dictation, give each student a strip, then tell them to circulate and get the answers from each other. Each student will have to speak to at least four others in order to correct the dictation. Using a different colour for each speaker, write on the board:

    A: What number do you have?

       B: I have number one.

    A: Can I see it, please?
      or
    A: Thanks anyway. I (already) have it.

Note: Although some teachers may feel that they are too traditional, dictations can be successful if they are short, if there is real communication between the teacher and the students, and if the number of repetitions is adequate. Dictations provide listening practice that students need in order to speak with confidence, and should be a teaching rather than a testing activity. Teacher-to-student dictations should be balanced with more student-centred activities like pair dictations or discussions, with much more class time spent on the latter.

Puzzle Review*

Don't do this activity on the same day as the Chop and Scramble activity. Put students into groups (page 7). Give each group a set of **cut up pictures and single words saved from the Chop and Scramble activity**, and have them put the dialogue together. Make them do it more than once. Have the groups read the dialogue to you. Assist with pronunciation.

When the students are ready for it, introduce related phrases on the board, such as:

    A: Is this okay?

        B: Yes, it is.
          or
        B: No, it isn't.

    A: I think this goes here.

        B: I (don't) think that's right.

Pair Dictations*

This exercise provides listening and speaking practice in a relaxed setting, and helps students connect spoken and written language. **Worksheets** are provided in each chapter. Give out all of the A sheets on one side of the class and all of the B sheets on the other. Let students choose, but ask them to work with partners that they haven't worked with yet that day. Have the students take turns dictating the dialogue to each other. Monitor groups and help students with pronunciation. Have students compare their papers when they are finished.

Performing the Dialogue

At this point, you may want to elicit alternatives to the language I have chosen. Ask students what other expressions they have heard.

Put students in pairs and give them some practice time. Monitor and help students with pronunciation, then have students perform the dialogue in front of the class with little or no written help. Use any **props** that are available, and let the students use the **cut-up pictures** as cue cards.

In order to maintain focus, it's best to do half of the pairs before a break, especially if you have a large class. Finish when you return.

Extension Activities for Single Dialogues

Make New Sentences*

Worksheets are provided in each chapter. This exercise can be challenging for beginners. Use the dialogue as a guide, and give students grammatical clues. If you have a low class, do this exercise together on the board. For higher classes, let students work in pairs. Monitor pairs, and then have students write corrected answers on the board. Add your own sentences, including first, second, and third person, singular and plural examples. Have students read the sentences as a class, and then copy them.

The new sentences can be used in later review activities such as Blanks on the Board or Dictation Relays, so make sure you keep copies.

Vocabulary Lists*

Worksheets are provided in each chapter; the lists begin with easier words and end with more difficult ones. Vocabulary lists should be viewed as guides only—adjust them to suit the needs of the class and your dialect. For low classes, remove some of the items from the list. If you have a higher class and you feel some items are missing, add them to the vocabulary list. Also, see Appendix A for suggestions for teaching more basic vocabulary such as parts of the body, numbers, dates, names of countries, time, and food.

Write the vocabulary words on the board. As much as possible, elicit explanations for the vocabulary from students. This is a challenging exercise for beginners, so you will have to provide much of the material—illustrations and examples help. Write the explanations on the board. Next, elicit (or provide) each word's part of speech and write it on the board. When you are finished, read the vocabulary, have students repeat chorally, and then have students copy.

On subsequent days, use the vocabulary to write sentences, then a new dialogue or a narrative (see below). Subsequent to that, do some of the exercises under the Review Activities for Vocabulary section (page 14).

Vocabulary Sentence Jigsaw

Use the numbering method on page 7 to divide the class into four groups. Give each student a fresh copy of the **Vocabulary List and a piece of coloured card stock,** using a different colour for each group. Assign each group one quarter of the vocabulary words and have them write a sentence with each word. Write sentence patterns on the board to assist students. Monitor and ensure the sentences are correct. When they are finished, ask students to form new groups of four people each; these groups will have one person from each of the original four colour groups. Monitor the new groups as students copy each others' sentences. Keep a copy of the sentences for later use as material for various review activities (pages 14 - 18).

New and Related Dialogue*

Elicit another, related dialogue from the students using another, related situation that your students may encounter, and write the dialogue on the board. For example, write a dialogue for bargaining when you teach the chapter on shopping. Ask students what language they need in their daily lives, and discuss any relevant cultural issues. Use local examples and words from the vocabulary lists. *This is where you can add material that may not be covered in the pictures and where you can customize the content to suit your students' needs.* Have a plan before you start.

When you are finished, have students copy the new dialogue into their notebooks. Have students read the dialogue as a class, and then practice it in pairs (pages 5 and 6). Save the dialogue for later use as material for various review activities (pages 14 - 18).

Narrative*

Use a dialogue to elicit a narrative about the characters. Write the narrative on the board as the students dictate, expanding and developing where necessary. Use local examples and words from the vocabulary lists, and have students give the characters names.

When you have finished writing, read the first phrase of the narrative as you run your hand below the words, then have the students repeat as a class. Continue this way until you have read the whole narrative, and then have each student read a sentence individually. This exercise will help students connect written and spoken language.

When you're finished, have the students copy the narrative into their notebooks. Narratives can be used to focus on a particular aspect of English, such as verbs or sentence stress. Ask students to identify all the verbs, for example. Save a copy of the narrative for later use as material for various review activities (pages 14 - 18). For further review, make a pair dictation from the narrative or write a question for each statement it contains and have students answer.

Discussion*

Discussion worksheets are provided in each chapter. Adjust them to make them more appropriate for your class, if necessary. Put students in groups of three or four (page 7). Elicit explanations for new vocabulary and for questions as needed, and then let the groups work through the questions on their own. Write phrases on the board to assist students. Monitor groups and record errors for later correction activities (page 19). Once students have finished, go through the questions in front of the class, but don't overdo it. It is unnecessary to repeat everything that has been said, and better to leave students wanting more.

Review Activities for Vocabulary

It is not necessary to do all of the activities for each chapter. Give students a couple of minutes to study before commencing activities, and then have them close their books. For putting students in groups, see page 7.

Vocabulary Pick-Up Cards*

Defining vocabulary can be quite challenging for beginning students, so this is a good activity to start with, because the teacher gives the definition and the students are only required to listen. Listening to the teacher's definition should help students with subsequent activities.

Write about 20 **vocabulary words on cards**, using the grid on page 157. Put the cards face up on a table and have the students gather around it. Call out a definition. Students try to pick up the corresponding card. The student with the most cards at the end wins the game.

Variation: Divide the class into two or more groups and use two or more sets of cards.

Tic Tac Toe*

Draw a nine-square grid on the board, and write a vocabulary word in each square. Put a challenging word in the middle square. Divide the class into two teams. The first team chooses a square, then must define the word and use it in a sentence. If they can't do it, the other team gets a chance. Teams take turns, and the first team to get three squares in a row wins. Make sure all of the students participate.

Zero Prep Vocabulary Test

Divide the class and the board in two. Give each team **about six small pieces of card stock**, then tell them to go through their notebooks and choose vocabulary words to test the other team. They can use the dialogues or any other material as a source for vocabulary. Have them write each word on a piece of card stock. Monitor and ensure that both teams do not choose the same words. Once they have finished, team one gives their first word to team two, and that team must define the word and then use it in a sentence. Have the teams take turns, and ensure all members participate. Give one point for each definition and one point for each sentence. Use more than two teams for higher classes.

This is a good game to use if you have just returned from holidays, because it gives you a chance to look through the students' notebooks to see what the substitute teacher has done in your absence. If you are a substitute teacher, this activity gives you a chance to see the material the class has covered, so you can quickly assess its level.

Vocabulary Board Game*

Use **the board game grid** on page 158. Write a different vocabulary word in each square. Put students into groups of four and hand out **a game, some markers, and a die for each group**. Students take turns rolling the die. When they land on a square, they must use the word in a sentence. Write some sentence patterns on the board to help students, and monitor groups.

Password

Let students study for a few minutes before beginning this activity. Place a chair with its back against the board, and have a volunteer sit in the chair. If students are reluctant to come forward, promise volunteers easy words. Write a vocabulary word on the board so that the volunteer can't see it. Have the other students give the volunteer clues until he or she guesses the correct word. Write phrases on the board to assist students with explanations. Have the volunteer choose the next student to sit in the chair. When the activity is finished, have students copy the phrases from the board.

Sticky Note Mingle

Write the vocabulary words on **sticky notes**. Make sure you have one for each student and a couple left over for early finishers. Let students study for a few minutes before beginning this activity. Stick the notes on the students' backs. (Check first to see is this action is culturally appropriate. If it isn't, it's best to choose another activity.) Have students circulate and give each other clues so they can guess their vocabulary words. Write phrases on the board to assist students with explanations. Have them copy the phrases from the board when the activity is finished.

Vocabulary Groups

This activity is more difficult than the Vocabulary Board Game. You will need **several sets of about 20 vocabulary cards**, one for each group. The cards can be made using the grid on page 157. Model the game with some higher students. Place a stack of cards face down on the table. The first student takes a card. If the student can explain the word, the student keeps the card. If not, another student can try to explain the word and take the card. Students take turns. The player with the most cards at the end of the game wins. Put students in groups of three or four, give each group a stack of cards, and monitor them while they play the game.

Variation: Have students use the vocabulary word in a sentence as well.

Review Activities for Multiple Dialogues

These activities are for reviewing three or more dialogues at a time. Activities are in approximate order of difficulty. It's not necessary to do every exercise in this section. For putting students in groups, see page 7.

Some of these activities can also be used to review material from the Extension Activities section, such as Making New Sentences, Vocabulary Sentence Jigsaw, New and Related Dialogues, and Narratives.

Some classes may not like to keep score while playing games, so you may want to alter the rules.

Dialogue Pick-Up Cards*

This is an easy listening activity for low classes. Cut out each picture from three dialogues, mix them up, and spread the **27 cards** face up on a table. Gather the students around. Call out a line of dialogue at random, speaking at normal speed with normal linking, reductions, intonation, and so on. Make it challenging for students. Have students pick up the corresponding card. The student with the most cards at the end wins.

Some pictures lend themselves better to this activity than others—you may want to eliminate pictures that might cause confusion.

Variation: Divide the class into two or more groups and use two or more sets of cards.

Reading Board Game*

This activity is for lower classes. Write lines from three dialogues or from the Extension Activities section onto the board game grid provided on page 158. Do this in random order, so students have to read the lines rather than relying on memory.

You will need **one die and one game board for each group, and a marker for each student**. Use the coloured strip method on page 7 to put one higher student in each group of three or four students. Students roll the dice, move their markers, and then read the lines that they land on. Let the higher students help their peers.

Drawing Game*

Give the students a couple of minutes to study three dialogues, and then have them close their books. Divide the class and the board in two (or more). Have a volunteer from each team come to the board. Give each volunteer a different, random **picture** from the dialogues. Some pictures lend themselves better to this activity than others. Choose carefully.

Stand facing the class as you show the pictures to the volunteers and have them look over your shoulder, so the other students can't see. Have the volunteers reproduce the picture on the board. The first team to correctly guess their line of dialogue gets a point. When the first two players are finished, they choose the next two players to draw. Continue until each student has had a turn at the board. The team with the most points wins.

Blanks on the Board*

This game used to be known as "Hangman," but that is not a good name to use for obvious reasons. Give students a couple of minutes to study three chapters, and then have them close their books. Divide the class into two or three teams. Write blanks on the board to represent each letter in a line of dialogue or a phrase from the Extension Activities section.

Have the first team guess a letter. If they guess correctly, write the letter in the corresponding blank and let the team have another turn. If the letter they guess is not in the line of dialogue, write it at the bottom of the board and allow the next team to have a turn. Do several lines at random. Award a point when a team completes a line. The team with the most points wins. Ensure that all team members participate.

Team Test

Divide the board and the class in two. Give students a couple of minutes to study three dialogues, and then have them close their books. Give each team a **picture card**. Choose carefully. Each team must write the corresponding line of dialogue on the board, and then read it aloud. Allow any correct answer. Give each team about six turns and ensure that all team members participate. Ultimately, the students should be able to produce a line of dialogue, randomly and out of context, from a picture cue.

Make New Sentences Review*

Write phrases from three chapters of the Make New Sentences section on the **cards** provided on page 157. Add your own phrases if you feel they are needed. For example, if you are reviewing "I'd like……..," you may want to add "He'd like………." as well. Put students in at least two groups and give each group a section of the board and a card. Have each group make as many sentences as they can on the board with their card. Grammatical prompts will help most students. You may want to use a **stop watch or egg timer**. Make sure everyone participates.

Dialogue Exchange 17

Award one point for each correct sentence. Repeat with additional cards. The group with the most sentences in the end wins. Have students read and then copy all of the sentences from the board when the game is finished.

Dictation Relay

Give students a couple of minutes to study three dialogues, and then have them close their books. Divide students into teams of four. Have the students go to four stations in the classroom, with one student from each team at each station. Make sure the stations are far apart. Use the hallway if appropriate. Give each student at the first station a different **line of dialogue written on card stock**.

The students at the first station must walk to the second station and whisper their lines of dialogue into their teammates' ears. The first students must not show their line of dialogue to the second students. The second students whisper their sentences into the ears of the third students. The third students whisper into the ears of the fourth students, who write the sentences on the board. The first team to correctly complete the relay wins. If any mistakes occur, students must correct them as a relay. That is, student four cannot speak directly to student one. Repeat the activity with additional sentences.

Position four requires strong students. Use the coloured strip method on page 7 and give the higher students the same colour so they end up on different teams. This activity can also be used to review material from the Extension Activities section.

Variation: Follow the same procedure as above, but use **picture cards** instead of lines of dialogue. This version of the relay is more difficult and will also require strong students in position one.

Stations

Once you have taught three or four dialogues, you can set up stations to review them. Record each dialogue and place one recorded dialogue at each station. Put students in groups and have them start at different stations, listening to the dialogues and then recording themselves. Students move clockwise through the stations at their own pace. You will need **at least three recording devices**. If you have a large class you will need more than one recording device at each station, so students don't have to wait. Stations can also be used to review material from the Extension Activities section.

Variation: Do a puzzle activity at each station, instead of a listening activity. Use a different dialogue at each station. You will need one or more sets of **cut-up pictures and single cut-up words** at each station, depending on the size of your class. Have the students move through the stations and put the dialogues together. Monitor, have the students read to you, and help them with pronunciation.

Correction

Blackboard Correction*

Write down some of the grammatical errors that the students make in class. During a break, copy the errors onto the board. Using a different colour of ink, elicit corrections from the students. Red ink is not recommended. Don't identify the student who made the error, and don't overwhelm them with too many examples; four or five is probably enough for a start. If the same errors keep coming up, keep writing them on the board. Do this activity regularly and make sure you catch every student eventually. When you're finished, have the students copy the corrected errors into their notebooks. (If you have students who are not making errors, send them for reassessment. They are in the wrong class.)

Correction activities are especially important after discussions—otherwise, students just practice their errors. Following up with correction will help students see the value of discussions, and you will begin to see real improvements in their speaking skills after a few weeks.

This activity may be a bit harsh for the first few classes. Save it for when the students are more comfortable with the language and with each other. Ensure that students understand that making errors is a necessary part of learning.

It is important to smile at all times, especially when you're correcting students. Creating a supportive, positive atmosphere that students will return to is more important than the finer points of English grammar. If students get frustrated, commiserate—English really is a difficult language for many. Always balance correction with positive reinforcement.

Correction Cards*

Alternatively, copy the students' errors onto **cards** using the grid on page 157. Number the cards. Put the students in groups and give each a set of cards. Have the students go through the cards and decide how the errors should be corrected. Monitor their progress. When they have finished, have students write corrected sentences on the board, then have the class copy all of the corrections from the board into their notebooks.

These cards can be saved up and used for review or used with subsequent classes.

*These activities can be adapted for one-on-one tutoring.

Dialogue Exchange 19

Dialogue Exchange 20

The Dialogues

Dialogue Exchange 22

Dialogue One: Giving Personal Information

Write the words for the dialogue under each picture.

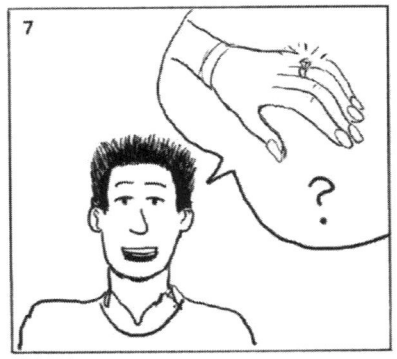

Dialogue Exchange 23

Dialogue One: Giving Personal Information

Hello, my name is _____.
It's nice to meet you. I'm _____.
Where are you from?
I'm from Mexico. What about you?
I'm from China. What are you doing in _____?
I'm a nurse.
Really. Are you married?
Yes, and I have two children.
That's wonderful.

Dialogue Exchange 24

Dialogue One: Giving Personal Information

Listen as your teacher reads. Mark the dialogue for sentence stress, intonation, linking, and reductions.

A: Hello, my name is_____.

B: It's nice to meet you. I'm _____.

A: Where are you from?

B: I'm from Mexico. What about you?

A: I'm from China. What are you doing in _____?

B: I'm a nurse.

A: Really. Are you married?

B: Yes, and I have two children.

A: That's wonderful.

Please say that again.
How do you spell that?

A

Dialogue One: Giving Personal Information

Read while your partner writes. Then write while your partner reads.

A: Hello, my name is_____.

B: _____

A: Where are you from?

B: _____

A: I'm from China. What are you doing in _____?

B: _____

A: Really. Are you married?

B: _____

A: That's wonderful.

When you are finished, look at your partner's paper. Is it the same as your paper?

Dialogue Exchange 26

Please say that again.
How do you spell that?

B

Dialogue One: Giving Personal Information

Write while your partner reads. Then read while your partner writes.

A: _____

B: It's nice to meet you. I'm _____.

A: _____

B: I'm from Mexico. What about you?

A: _____

B: I'm a nurse.

A: _____

B: Yes, and I have two children.

A: _____

When you are finished, look at your partner's paper. Is it the same as your paper?

Dialogue One: Giving Personal Information

Make new sentences. Use the dialogue to help you.

1. _____from _____.

2. Where _____ from?

3. I'm a _____.

4. Are you _____?

5. I have_____.

6. That's _____.

Dialogue Exchange 28

Dialogue One: Giving Personal Information

Vocabulary

1. family
2. husband
3. wife
4. mother/father
5. son/daughter
6. brother
7. sister
8. parent
9. child(ren)
10. grandfather/grandmother
11. relative
12. uncle/aunt
13. cousin
14. boyfriend/girlfriend
15. friend
16. married
17. single
18. separated/divorced
19. widowed
20. teacher
21. student
22. doctor
23. secretary
24. businessman/businesswoman
25. cook
26. What is your phone number?
27. What is your address?

Dialogue One: Giving Personal Information

Discussion

1. Where are you from? Is it a big city or a small town? Do you live there now? Do you miss it?

2. Tell us about your family. Do you have parents? Children? Do you have brothers and sisters? Aunts and uncles? Where do they live?

3. What are you doing here? Are you working, studying, or visiting? What is your job? Why are you learning English?

4. Is it easy to meet new people? Is it easier to meet people in small towns or big cities? Is this a friendly city? Where is a good place to meet people?

5. Is it okay to ask people if they are married when you first meet them? Why or why not? Does it matter where you meet them? Does it matter if they are the opposite sex?

See Appendix A on page 145 for additional teaching materials on this topic.

Dialogue Two: Asking For Help with English

Write the words for the dialogue under each picture.

Dialogue Exchange 31

Dialogue Two: Asking for Help with English

Excuse me. Can I ask you a question?
Sure, no problem.
I'm learning English. What is this called?
It's a guitar.
Can you say that again, more slowly?
It's a guitar.
How do you spell that, please?
G U I T A R
Thank you very much for your help.

Dialogue Two: Asking For Help with English

Listen as your teacher reads. Mark the dialogue for sentence stress, intonation, linking, and reductions.

A: Excuse me. Can I ask you a question?

B: Sure, no problem.

A: I'm learning English. What is this called?

B: It's a guitar.

A: Can you say that again, more slowly?

B: It's a guitar.

A: How do you spell that, please?

B: G-U-I-T-A-R.

A: Thank you very much for your help.

Please say that again.
How do you spell that?

A

Dialogue Two: Asking For Help with English

Read while your partner writes. Then write while your partner reads.

A: Excuse me. Can I ask you a question?

B: _____

A: I'm learning English. What is this called?

B: _____

A: Can you say that again, more slowly?

B: _____

A: How do you spell that, please?

B: _____

A: Thank you very much for your help.

When you are finished, look at your partner's paper. Is it the same as your paper?

Dialogue Exchange 34

Please say that again.
How do you spell that?

B

Dialogue Two: Asking For Help with English

Write while your partner reads. Then read while your partner writes.

A: _____

B: Sure, no problem.

A: _____

B: It's a guitar.

A: _____

B: It's a guitar.

A: _____

B: G-U-I-T-A-R.

A: _____

When you are finished, look at your partner's paper. Is it the same as your paper?

Dialogue Two: Asking For Help with English

Make new sentences. Use the dialogue to help you.

1. Can I ask _____?

2. I'm learning_____.

3. It's a _____.

4. Can you say _____?

5. How do you spell _____?

6. Thank you very much for _____.

Dialogue Two: Asking For Help with English

Vocabulary

1. read
2. write
3. listen
4. speak
5. understand
6. repeat
7. teach
8. learn
9. answer
10. mean
11. chair
12. table
13. desk
14. pen
15. pencil
16. eraser
17. book
18. notebook
19. dictionary
20. worksheet
21. classroom
22. door
23. window
24. floor
25. wall
26. (white)board
27. (tele)phone

Dialogue Two: Asking For Help with English

Discussion

1. What is difficult about learning English? Why? What is easy? Why?

2. What is the best way to learn vocabulary? Why?

3. Is it better to learn English with people or with a computer? Why?

4. Do you talk to English speakers sometimes? Where do you meet them? How can you meet more English speakers? Do they like to help you?

5. How can you get listening practice after class?

Dialogue Three: Ordering a meal

Write the words for the dialogue under each picture.

Dialogue Exchange 39

Dialogue Three: Ordering a Meal

Hello. Welcome.

I'd like a table for two, please.

This way, please. Here's a menu.

Thank you.

Are you ready to order?

We'll have a pizza, a juice, and a coffee.

Here you go. Can I get you anything else?

No thanks. Can I have the check, please?

Sure. I'll bring it.

Dialogue Three: Ordering a meal

Listen as your teacher reads. Mark the dialogue for sentence stress, intonation, linking, and reductions.

A: Hello. Welcome.

B: I'd like a table for two, please.

A: This way, please. Here's a menu.

B: Thank you.

A: Are you ready to order?

B: We'll have a pizza, a juice, and a coffee.

A: Here you go. Can I get you anything else?

B: No thanks. Can I have the check, please?

A: Sure. I'll bring it.

Please say that again.
How do you spell that?

A

Dialogue Three: Ordering a meal

Read while your partner writes. Then write while your partner reads.

A: Hello. Welcome.

B: _____

A: This way, please. Here's a menu.

B: _____

A: Are you ready to order?

B: _____

A: Here you go. Can I get you anything else?

B: _____

A: Sure. I'll bring it.

When you are finished, look at your partner's paper. Is it the same as your paper?

Dialogue Exchange 42

Please say that again.
How do you spell that?

B

Dialogue Three: Ordering a meal

Write while your partner reads. Then read while your partner writes.

A: _____

B: I'd like a table for two, please.

A: _____

B: Thank you.

A: _____

B: We'll have a pizza, a juice, and a coffee.

A: _____

B: No thanks. Can I have the check, please?

A: _____

When you are finished, look at your partner's paper. Is it the same as your paper?

Dialogue Three: Ordering a meal

Make new sentences. Use the dialogue to help you.

1. I'd like _____.

2. Here's _____.

3. Are you ready to _____?

4. Can I get you _____?

5. Can I have _____?

6. I'll bring _____.

Dialogue Three: Ordering a meal

Vocabulary

1. eat
2. drink
3. vegetable
4. fruit
5. meat
6. beef
7. pork
8. chicken
9. fish
10. egg
11. bread
12. rice
13. water
14. napkin
15. fork
16. knife
17. spoon
18. chopsticks
19. delicious
20. for here
21. to go
22. (for) delivery
23. (non)smoking
24. vegetarian
25. allergic to
26. hungry
27. full

Dialogue Three: Ordering a meal

Discussion

1. Would you rather eat in a restaurant or at home? Why? What can you cook? How many times a week do you eat in restaurants?

2. What is your favourite restaurant? Why? What do you order there?

3. What type of food do you like? Chinese? Mexican? Indian? Korean? Thai? Vegetarian? Seafood? Why?

4. Is there anything that you will not eat? What? Why won't you eat it?

5. Do you eat fast food? What is your favourite fast food restaurant? Why? How often do you go there? What do you order? Do they serve healthy food?

See Appendix A on page 145 for additional teaching materials on this topic.

Dialogue Four: Shopping

Write the words for the dialogue under each picture.

Dialogue Exchange 47

Dialogue Four: Shopping

Can I help you?

Yes, how much do these shoes cost?

They're fifty dollars.

Do you have them in size seven?

I think so. Have a seat, please. I'll check.

Here you go. Do you want to try them on?

They fit well. I like them. I'll take them.

Will that be cash or on your account?

I'll pay cash.

Dialogue Exchange 48

Dialogue Four: Shopping

Listen as your teacher reads. Mark the dialogue for sentence stress, intonation, linking, and reductions.

A: Can I help you?

B: Yes, how much do these shoes cost?

A: They're fifty dollars.

B: Do you have them in size seven?

A: I think so. Have a seat, please. I'll check.

A: Here you go. Do you want to try them on?

B: They fit well. I like them. I'll take them.

A: Will that be cash or on your account?

B: I'll pay cash.

Please say that again.
How do you spell that?

A

Dialogue Four: Shopping

Read while your partner writes. Then write while your partner reads.

A: Can I help you?

B: _____

A: They're fifty dollars.

B: _____

A: I think so. Have a seat, please. I'll check.

A: Here you go. Do you want to try them on?

B: _____

A: Will that be cash or on your account?

B: _____

When you are finished, look at your partner's paper. Is it the same as your paper?

Dialogue Exchange 50

Please say that again.
How do you spell that?

B

Dialogue Four: Shopping

Write while your partner reads. Then read while your partner writes.

A: _____

B: Yes, how much do these shoes cost?

A: _____

B: Do you have them in size seven?

A: _____

A: _____

B: They fit well. I like them. I'll take them.

A: _____

B: I'll pay cash.

When you are finished, look at your partner's paper. Is it the same as your paper?

Dialogue Exchange 51

Dialogue Four: Shopping

Make new sentences. Use the dialogue to help you.

1. How much do _____?

2. They're _____.

3. Do you have _____?

4. Do you want to _____?

5. I like _____.

6. I'll pay _____.

Dialogue Four: Shopping

Vocabulary

1. colour
2. red
3. blue
4. yellow
5. black
6. white
7. green
8. orange
9. purple
10. small/medium/large
11. long
12. short
13. light
14. dark
15. cheap
16. expensive
17. cashier
18. credit card
19. debit card
20. cheque
21. change
22. exchange
23. refund
24. receipt
25. credit note
26. I'm just looking.
27. What's your best price?

Dialogue Four: Shopping

Discussion

1. Do you like to shop? How often do you go shopping? What do you like to shop for? What do you not like to shop for?

2. What is your favourite place to shop here? Why? What can you buy? Is it cheap or expensive? Is there anything you can't buy here?

3. What is your favourite place to shop in the world? Why? What can you buy there? Is it cheaper or more expensive than here?

4. Would you rather shop in person or online? Why? What things do you buy online? What things do you buy in person? What sites do you like?

5. What are the best deals for clothes? For food? For household goods? For services?

See pages 145 - 146 and 148 for additional teaching suggestions for this topic.

Dialogue Five: Calling for Help in an Emergency

Write the words for the dialogue under each picture.

Dialogue Exchange 55

Dialogue Five: Calling for Help in an Emergency

Fire, police, or ambulance?

I need an ambulance, please.

What's the matter?

My mother feels sick. It's her heart.

What's your address?

It's 385 Fifth Street.

Is that a house or an apartment?

It's a house. How long will it take?

Don't worry. We'll be there right away.

Dialogue Five: Calling for Help in an Emergency

Listen as your teacher reads. Mark the dialogue for sentence stress, intonation, linking, and reductions.

A: Fire, police, or ambulance?

B: I need an ambulance, please.

A: What's the matter?

B: My mother feels sick. It's her heart.

A: What's your address?

B: It's 385 Fifth Street.

A: Is that a house or an apartment?

B: It's a house. How long will it take?

A: Don't worry. We'll be there right away.

Please say that again.
How do you spell that?

A

Dialogue Five: Calling for Help in an Emergency

Read while your partner writes. Then write while your partner reads.

A: Fire, police, or ambulance?

B: _____

A: What's the matter?

B: _____

A: What's your address?

B: _____

A: Is that a house or an apartment?

B: _____

A: Don't worry. We'll be there right away.

When you are finished, look at your partner's paper. Is it the same as your paper?

Please say that again.
How do you spell that?

B

Dialogue Five: Calling for Help in an Emergency

Write while your partner reads. Then read while your partner writes.

A: _____

B: I need an ambulance, please.

A: _____

B: My mother feels sick. It's her heart.

A: _____

B: It's 385 Fifth Street.

A: _____

B: It's a house. How long will it take?

A: _____

When you are finished, look at your partner's paper. Is it the same as your paper?

Dialogue Five: Calling for Help in an Emergency

Make new sentences. Use the dialogue to help you.

1. I need _____.

2. My mother feels _____.

3. What's your _____?

4. Is that a _____?

5. How long will _____?

6. We'll be there _____.

Dialogue Five: Calling for Help in an Emergency

Vocabulary

1. Help!
2. Watch out!
3. hospital
4. insurance
5. emergency
6. accident
7. pedestrian
8. car/truck/van/SUV/motorcycle
9. hit
10. hit-and-run
11. impaired
12. injury
13. blood
14. bruise
15. cut
16. broken (bone)
17. burn
18. dizzy
19. fever
20. sore
21. hurt
22. (un)conscious
23. robbery
24. steal
25. assault
26. break-in
27. on fire

Dialogue Five: Calling for Help in an Emergency

Discussion

1. Do you feel safe at home or away? Why or why not? What can you do to feel more safe?

2. Do you have to pay if you call an ambulance? How much? Do you have to pay if you go to an emergency ward in a hospital? How much? Do you have to pay if you go to a walk-in clinic? How much?

3. When should you call an ambulance? When should you go to an emergency ward? When should you go to a walk-in clinic?

4. When should you call the police? What is the emergency number? What is the non-emergency number? When should you not call the police?

5. What number can you call if you see an animal that is hurt? What will happen? What if it is your animal?

See Appendix A on page 149 for additional teaching materials on this topic.

Dialogue Six: Asking for Directions

Write the words for the dialogue under each picture.

Dialogue Exchange 63

Dialogue Six: Asking for Directions

Excuse me. Can I ask you a question?

Yes, can I help you find something?

Is there a grocery store near here?

Yes, turn right at the next intersection.

Okay, then what?

Then go straight for two blocks.

Uh huh.

It's beside the dentist, across from the pharmacy.

Thank you very much.

Dialogue Exchange 64

Dialogue Six: Asking for Directions

Listen as your teacher reads. Mark the dialogue for sentence stress, intonation, linking, and reductions.

A: Excuse me. Can I ask you a question?

B: Yes, can I help you find something?

A: Is there a grocery store near here?

B: Yes, turn right at the next intersection.

A: Okay, then what?

B: Then go straight for two blocks.

A: Uh huh.

B: It's beside the dentist, across from the pharmacy.

A: Thank you very much.

Please say that again.
How do you spell that?

A

Dialogue Six: Asking for Directions

Read while your partner writes. Then write while your partner reads.

A: Excuse me. Can I ask you a question?

B: _____

A: Is there a grocery store near here?

B: _____

A: Okay, then what?

B: _____

A: Uh huh.

B: _____

A: Thank you very much.

When you are finished, look at your partner's paper. Is it the same as your paper?

Dialogue Exchange 66

Please say that again.
How do you spell that?

B

Dialogue Six: Asking for Directions

Write while your partner reads. Then read while your partner writes.

A: _____

B: Yes, can I help you find something?

A: _____

B: Yes, turn right at the next intersection.

A: _____

B: Then go straight for two blocks.

A: _____

B: It's beside the dentist, across from the pharmacy.

A: _____

When you are finished, look at your partner's paper. Is it the same as your paper?

Dialogue Six: Asking for Directions

Make new sentences. Use the dialogue to help you.

1. Is there a _____ near here?

2. Turn right at _____.

3. Turn left at _____.

4. Go straight for _____.

5. It's beside _____.

6. It's across from _____.

Dialogue Six: Asking for Directions

Vocabulary

1. street
2. corner
3. sidewalk
4. crosswalk
5. traffic light
6. stop sign
7. shop
8. supermarket
9. department store
10. mall
11. church/temple/mosque/synagogue
12. office
13. government office
14. office building
15. restaurant
16. cafe
17. bar/night club
18. laundromat
19. hairdresser/barber
20. post office
21. gas station
22. bus station/train station
23. restroom/washroom/bathroom/toilet
24. Where is the nearest _____?
25. How far is it?
26. Can you draw me a map?
27. Where is _____ Street?

Dialogue Six: Asking for Directions

Discussion

1. Have you been lost in a strange city? What did you do?

2. Would you rather use a map or ask for directions? Why?

3. Are things easy to find in this city? Why or why not?

4. Do you use the internet for directions? Which sites do you use? Are they helpful?

5. Have you used GPS? Do you like it? Is it easy to use? How much does GPS cost?

Dialogue Seven: Renting an Apartment

Write the words for the dialogue under each picture.

Dialogue Exchange 71

Dialogue Seven: Renting an Apartment

Hello, I'm calling about the apartment.
Yes, it's $600 plus utilities.
How many bedrooms does it have?
It has one bedroom and one bathroom.
Where is it located?
It's at 6888 Main Street. It's near the park.
Do I have to sign a lease?
No, month to month is okay.
I'd like to see the apartment, please.

Dialogue Seven: Renting an Apartment

Listen as your teacher reads. Mark the dialogue for sentence stress, intonation, linking, and reductions.

A: Hello, I'm calling about the apartment.

B: Yes, it's $600 plus utilities.

A: How many bedrooms does it have?

B: It has one bedroom and one bathroom.

A: Where is it located?

B: It's at 6888 Main Street. It's near the park.

A: Do I have to sign a lease?

B: No, month to month is okay.

A: I'd like to see the apartment, please.

Please say that again.
How do you spell that?

A

Dialogue Seven: Renting an Apartment

Read while your partner writes. Then write while your partner reads.

A: Hello, I'm calling about the apartment.

B: _____

A: How many bedrooms does it have?

B: _____

A: Where is it located?

B: _____

A: Do I have to sign a lease?

B: _____

A: I'd like to see the apartment, please.

When you are finished, look at your partner's paper. Is it the same as your paper?

Dialogue Exchange 74

Please say that again.
How do you spell that?

B

Dialogue Seven: Renting an Apartment

Write while your partner reads. Then read while your partner writes.

A: _____

B: Yes, it's $600 plus utilities.

A: _____

B: It has one bedroom and one bathroom.

A: _____

B: It's at 6888 Main Street. It's near the park.

A: _____

B: No, month to month is okay.

A: _____

When you are finished, look at your partner's paper. Is it the same as your paper?

Dialogue Seven: Renting an Apartment

Make new sentences. Use the dialogue to help you.

1. I'm calling about _____.

2. It's _____, plus _____.

3. How many _____ does it have?

4. It has _____.

5. It's at _____ near _____.

6. Do I have to _____?

Dialogue Exchange 76

Dialogue Seven: Renting an Apartment

Vocabulary

1. heat
2. air conditioning
3. electricity
4. (hot/cold) water
5. cable
6. internet
7. laundry
8. kitchen
9. living room
10. dining room
11. balcony/patio
12. bathtub
13. shower
14. hardwood floor
15. carpet
16. tile
17. curtains/blinds
18. (un)furnished
19. view
20. security
21. damage deposit
22. condominium
23. apartment building
24. location
25. pet
26. show
27. What floor is it on?

Dialogue Seven: Renting an Apartment

Discussion

1. How much do you have to pay when you move into a rented house or apartment? Do you get some of the money back when you move out?

2. What is usually included when you rent an apartment? What is usually extra? How much extra do you have to pay?

3. What is shared accommodation? Is it common where you are from? Would you live in shared accommodation? Why or why not?

4. Do you think it would be easy to be a landlord? Why or why not? Would you do it?

5. What are the most important questions when you are renting an apartment? Write five questions.

See page 145 - 146 for additional teaching suggestions for this topic.

Dialogue Eight: Taking the Bus

Write the words for the dialogue under each picture.

Dialogue Exchange 79

Dialogue Eight: Taking the Bus

Do you go downtown?
I go to Granville. You can transfer there.
Which bus do I transfer to?
Number 20 Granville.
Can you please call out Granville Street?
Sure, no problem.
Granville Street next.
Thanks. See you later.
You're welcome. Have a nice day.

Dialogue Eight: Taking the Bus

Listen as your teacher reads. Mark the dialogue for sentence stress, intonation, linking, and reductions.

A: Do you go downtown?

B: I go to Granville. You can transfer there.

A: Which bus do I transfer to?

B: Number 20 Granville.

A: Can you please call out Granville Street?

B: Sure. No problem.

B: Granville Street next.

A: Thanks. See you later.

B: You're welcome. Have a nice day.

Please say that again.
How do you spell that?

A

Dialogue Eight: Taking the Bus

Read while your partner writes. Then write while your partner reads.

A: Do you go downtown?

B: _____

A: Which bus do I transfer to?

B: _____

A: Can you please call out Granville Street?

B: _____

B: _____

A: Thanks. See you later.

B: _____

When you are finished, look at your partner's paper. Is it the same as your paper?

Please say that again.
How do you spell that?

B

Dialogue Eight: Taking the Bus

Write while your partner reads. Then read while your partner writes.

A: _____

B: I go to Granville. You can transfer there.

A: _____

B: Number 20 Granville.

A: _____

B: Sure. No problem.

B: Granville Street next.

A: _____

B: You're welcome. Have a nice day.

When you are finished, look at your partner's paper. Is it the same as your paper?

Dialogue Eight: Taking the Bus

Make new sentences. Use the dialogue to help you.

1. Do you go _____?

2. I go to _____.

3. Which _____ do I _____?

4. Can you please _____?

5. See you _____.

6. Have a _____.

Dialogue Eight: Taking the Bus

Vocabulary

1. driver
2. passenger
3. sit
4. stand
5. get on/get off
6. move back
7. step down
8. fare
9. ticket
10. (transit) pass
11. subway
12. ferry
13. train
14. express bus
15. aisle
16. (front/back) door
17. emergency exit
18. (courtesy) seat
19. cord
20. steps
21. bus stop
22. station
23. route
24. schedule
25. Which bus goes to…..?
26. How often does the bus go to…….?
27. When is the next bus to…….?

Dialogue Eight: Taking the Bus

Discussion

1. Do you take the bus? How often? Which bus? Is the service good?

2. Do you take rapid transit? Do you like it? Which city has the best rapid transit?

3. Do you feel safe taking the bus at night? What can you do to feel safer?

4. Is there a website with information on transit? What is the web address? What information does it have?

5. When should you give your seat to another passenger? What is polite behaviour on the bus? What is rude behaviour?

Dialogue Nine: Making Appointments

Write the words for the dialogue under each picture.

Dialogue Exchange 87

Dialogue Nine: Making Appointments

Hello, First Street Clinic.
Hi, this is _____. I'd like to see the doctor.
How about Wednesday, July 17th at 2:00 p.m.?
I'm sorry. I'm busy on Wednesday.
Okay, how about Friday, July 19th at 3:00 p.m.?
Sure, that's good.
Please bring your medical card.
Okay, see you on Friday at 3:00.
See you then. Bye.

Dialogue Nine: Making Appointments

Listen as your teacher reads. Mark the dialogue for sentence stress, intonation, linking, and reductions.

A: Hello, First Street Clinic.

B: Hi, this is _____. I'd like to see the doctor.

A: How about Wednesday, July 17th at 2:00 p.m.?

B: I'm sorry. I'm busy on Wednesday.

A: Okay, how about Friday, July 19th at 3:00 p.m.?

B: Sure, that's good.

A: Please bring your medical card.

B: Okay, see you on Friday at 3:00.

A: See you then. Bye.

Please say that again.
How do you spell that?

A

Dialogue Nine: Making Appointments

Read while your partner writes. Then write while your partner reads.

A: Hello, First Street Clinic.

B: _____

A: How about Wednesday, July 17th at 2:00 p.m.?

B: _____

A: Okay, how about Friday, July 19th at 3:00 p.m.?

B: _____

A: Please bring your medical card.

B: _____

A: See you then. Bye.

When you are finished, look at your partner's paper. Is it the same as your paper?

Please say that again.
How do you spell that?

B

Dialogue Nine: Making Appointments

Write while your partner reads. Then read while your partner writes.

A: _____

B: Hi, this is _____. I'd like to see the doctor.

A: _____

B: I'm sorry. I'm busy on Wednesday.

A: _____

B: Sure, that's good.

A: _____

B: Okay, see you on Friday at 3:00.

A: _____

When you are finished, look at your partner's paper. Is it the same as your paper?

Dialogue Nine: Making Appointments

Make new sentences. Use the dialogue to help you.

1. This is _____.

2. How about _____?

3. I'm busy _____.

4. Sure, that's _____.

5. Please bring _____.

6. See you on _____.

Dialogue Exchange 92

Dialogue Nine: Making Appointments

Vocabulary

1. four o'clock
2. 5:00 a.m./5:00 p.m.
3. half past three/three thirty
4. a quarter to six/a quarter past six
5. second
6. minute
7. hour
8. twenty to twelve/twenty past twelve
9. noon/midnight
10. morning/afternoon/evening
11. watch/clock
12. today/tonight
13. tomorrow
14. yesterday
15. day after tomorrow
16. day before yesterday
17. a month ago
18. this week
19. next week
20. last week
21. first/second/third/fourth
22. date
23. late/early
24. on time
25. What time is it?
26. Do you have the time?
27. When will it be ready?

Dialogue Nine: Making Appointments

Discussion

1. Is it okay to be late for doctors' appointments? Should you call if you will be late? Should you call if you are meeting a friend? A business associate? What if it is a job interview?

2. If you forget a doctor's appointment, do you have to pay? What if you forget about a haircut? How much notice (time) should you give if you have to cancel an appointment?

3. What time do you get up in the morning during the week? On the weekend? Are you an early bird or a night owl? Which is better?

4. If someone invites you to their house for dinner at 6:30 p.m., when should you arrive? When should you leave? If someone asks you over for a party at 9:00 p.m., should you call if you're going to be 20 minutes late?

5. How do people in your culture feel about being on time? Are they the same as most English speakers?

See Appendix A, page 150 for additional teaching materials on this topic.

Dialogue Ten: Opening a Bank Account

Write the words for the dialogue under each picture.

Dialogue Exchange 95

Dialogue Ten: Opening a Bank Account

I'd like to open an account, please.

Okay. Can I see some ID?

Here's my passport.

I need something with your address.

Here's my driver's licence.

Okay. Please fill out this form.

Will I get an ATM card?

Yes. How much would you like to deposit?

I'll put in $100.

Dialogue Exchange 96

Dialogue Ten: Opening a Bank Account

Listen as your teacher reads. Mark the dialogue for sentence stress, intonation, linking, and reductions.

A: I'd like to open an account, please.

B: Okay. Can I see some ID?

A: Here's my passport.

B: I need something with your address.

A: Here's my driver's license.

B: Okay. Please fill out this form.

A: Will I get an ATM card?

B: Yes. How much would you like to deposit?

A: I'll put in $100.

Please say that again.
How do you spell that?

A

Dialogue Ten: Opening a Bank Account

Read while your partner writes. Then write while your partner reads.

A: I'd like to open an account, please.

B: _____

A: Here's my passport.

B: _____

A: Here's my driver's license.

B: _____

A: Will I get an ATM card?

B: _____

A: I'll put in $100.

When you are finished, look at your partner's paper. Is it the same as your paper?

Dialogue Exchange 98

Please say that again.
How do you spell that?

B

Dialogue Ten: Opening a Bank Account

Write while your partner reads. Then read while your partner writes.

A: _____

B: Okay. Can I see some ID?

A: _____

B: I need something with your address.

A: _____

B: Okay. Please fill out this form.

A: _____

B: Yes. How much would you like to deposit?

A: _____

When you are finished, look at your partner's paper. Is it the same as your paper?

Dialogue Ten: Opening a Bank Account

Make new sentences. Use the dialogue to help you.

1. Can I see _____?

2. I need something with _____.

3. Please fill out _____.

4. Will I get a(n) _____?

5. How much would you like to _____?

6. I'll put in _____.

Dialogue Exchange 100

Dialogue Ten: Opening a Bank Account

Vocabulary

1. cash
2. cheque
3. travelers' cheques
4. change some money
5. cash a cheque
6. deposit
7. withdraw
8. debit card
9. credit card
10. (chequing) account
11. coin/bill
12. change
13. penny/nickel/dime/quarter/buck/loonie/toonie/
14. pound/quid/pence
15. ATM
16. teller
17. fee
18. safe deposit box
19. foreign exchange
20. exchange rate
21. interest rate
22. loan
23. borrow
24. line of credit
25. mortgage
26. investment
27. term deposit

Dialogue Ten: Opening a Bank Account

Discussion

1. How many bank accounts do you have? How many credit cards? Is it good to have more than one bank? Why or why not?

2. What bank(s) do you use? Is the service good? Which bank is the best? Which bank is the worst?

3. Do you use online banking or do you go in person? Which do you like better? Why?

4. Would you like to work in a bank? Why or why not?

5. Is it better to invest your money in a bank, in the stock market, or in real estate?

Dialogue Eleven: Applying for a Job

Write the words for the dialogue under each picture.

Dialogue Exchange 103

Dialogue Eleven: Applying for a Job

Hello, I'd like to apply for a job.
Do you have any experience?
Yes, I worked for five years in Italy.
Do you have a certificate?
Yes, it's in the envelope with my résumé.
Okay, please fill out this application.
Thank you.
We'll have an interview later.
That's great! I look forward to it.

Dialogue Exchange 104

Dialogue Eleven: Applying for a Job

Listen as your teacher reads. Mark the dialogue for sentence stress, intonation, linking, and reductions.

A: Hello, I'd like to apply for a job.

B: Do you have any experience?

A: Yes, I worked for five years in Italy.

B: Do you have a certificate?

A: Yes, it's in the envelope with my résumé.

B: Okay, please fill out this application.

A: Thank you.

B: We'll have an interview later.

A: That's great! I look forward to it.

Please say that again.
How do you spell that?

A

Dialogue Eleven: Applying for a Job

Read while your partner writes. Then write while your partner reads.

A: Hello, I'd like to apply for a job.

B: _____

A: Yes, I worked for five years in Italy.

B: _____

A: Yes, it's in the envelope with my résumé.

B: _____

A: Thank you.

B: _____

A: That's great! I look forward to it.

When you are finished, look at your partner's paper. Is it the same as your paper?

Please say that again.
How do you spell that?

B

Dialogue Eleven: Applying for a Job

Write while your partner reads. Then read while your partner writes.

A: _____

B: Do you have any experience?

A: _____

B: Do you have a certificate?

A: _____

B: Okay, please fill out this application.

A: _____

B: We'll have an interview later.

A: _____

When you are finished, look at your partner's paper. Is it the same as your paper?

Dialogue Eleven: Applying for a Job

Make new sentences. Use the dialogue to help you.

1. I'd like to apply for _____.

2. Do you have any _____?

3. I worked for _____.

4. It's in the _____.

5. We'll have _____.

6. I look forward to _____.

Dialogue Exchange 108

Dialogue Eleven: Applying for a Job

Vocabulary

1. résumé/CV
2. reference
3. certificate
4. diploma
5. degree
6. (on-the-job) training
7. work experience
8. volunteer experience
9. internship
10. probation
11. hire
12. fire
13. quit
14. lay off
15. job
16. work
17. shift
18. salary
19. wage
20. paycheque
21. boss
22. worker
23. co-worker
24. employer
25. employee
26. holiday
27. day off

Dialogue Eleven: Applying for a Job

Discussion

1. Have you applied for a job? Was it easy or difficult? Were you nervous? Did you get the job?

2. Should you make an appointment or just show up? What should you bring with you?

3. How important are certificates and experience? Where can you get certificates? Where can you get experience?

4. Would you rather have a job or have your own business? Why? Is it easy to start a business here? Why or why not?

5. What are the most important things when you are applying for a job?

Dialogue Twelve: Joining a Community Centre

Write the words for the dialogue under each picture.

Dialogue Twelve: Joining a Community Centre

I'd like to take a photography course.
Which one do you want?
This one here.
That's $50. Is there anything else?
Yes, I'd like a monthly gym membership.
Do you want to use the swimming pool?
How much does it cost?
It's $20 extra.
That's all right. I'll take it.

Dialogue Exchange 112

Dialogue Twelve: Joining a Community Centre

Listen as your teacher reads. Mark the dialogue for sentence stress, intonation, linking, and reductions.

A: I'd like to take a photography course.

B: Which one do you want?

A: This one here.

B: That's $50. Is there anything else?

A: Yes, I'd like a monthly gym membership.

B: Do you want to use the swimming pool?

A: How much does it cost?

B: It's $20 extra.

A: That's all right. I'll take it.

Please say that again.
How do you spell that?

A

Dialogue Twelve: Joining a Community Centre

Read while your partner writes. Then write while your partner reads.

A: I'd like to take a photography course.

B: _____

A: This one here.

B: _____

A: Yes, I'd like a monthly gym membership.

B: _____

A: How much does it cost?

B: _____

A: That's all right. I'll take it.

When you are finished, look at your partner's paper. Is it the same as your paper?

Please say that again.
How do you spell that?

B

Dialogue Twelve: Joining a Community Centre

Write while your partner reads. Then read while your partner writes.

A: _____

B: Which one do you want?

A: _____

B: That's $50. Is there anything else?

A: _____

B: Do you want to use the swimming pool?

A: _____

B: It's $20 extra.

A: _____

When you are finished, look at your partner's paper. Is it the same as your paper?

Dialogue Exchange 115

Dialogue Twelve: Joining a Community Centre

Make new sentences. Use the dialogue to help you.

1. I'd like to _____.

2. Which one do you _____?

3. Is there _____?

4. I'd like a _____.

5. Do you want to use the_____?

6. _____ extra.

Dialogue Exchange 116

Dialogue Twelve: Joining a Community Centre

Vocabulary

1. gym
2. swimming pool
3. sauna
4. hot tub
5. fitness equipment
6. exercise bike
7. treadmill
8. weights
9. exercise
10. work out
11. swim
12. dance
13. hike
14. ski
15. skate
16. cycle
17. bowl
18. (do) aerobics
19. (do) yoga
20. (play) hockey
21. (play) basketball
22. (play) football
23. (play) baseball
24. (play) soccer
25. (play) chess
26. (play) mah jong
27. club

Dialogue Twelve: Joining a Community Centre

Discussion

1. Do you belong to a community centre or a gym? Which one? Do you like it? How often do you go? What do you do there? Do you like the people there? Do you like the facilities?

2. Name all of the fitness centres near here. Which ones are best? Why? How much do they cost to join?

3. How can you keep fit without going to the gym? Are there other clubs or groups that you can join?

4. Where can you take photography courses? Cooking courses? Other hobbies?

5. What do you do in your spare time? What did you do in your spare time when you were younger?

Dialogue Thirteen: Checking in at the Airport

Write the words for the dialogue under each picture.

Dialogue Exchange 119

Dialogue Thirteen: Checking in at the Airport

Can I see your ticket and passport, please?
Here they are.
Put your bags on the scale, please.
This is my carry-on bag.
Would you like a window seat?
No, I'd rather have an aisle seat, please.
Go to Gate 5 one hour before your flight.
Where is it?
Go through Security and turn right.

Dialogue Thirteen: Checking in at the Airport

Listen as your teacher reads. Mark the dialogue for sentence stress, intonation, linking, and reductions.

A: Can I see your ticket and passport, please?

B: Here they are.

A: Put your bags on the scale, please.

B: This is my carry-on bag.

A: Would you like a window seat?

B: No, I'd rather have an aisle seat, please.

A: Go to Gate 5 one hour before your flight.

B: Where is it?

A: Go through Security and turn right.

Please say that again.
How do you spell that?

A

Dialogue Thirteen: Checking in at the Airport

Read while your partner writes. Then write while your partner reads.

A: Can I see your ticket and passport, please?

B: _____

A: Put your bags on the scale, please.

B: _____

A: Would you like a window seat?

B: _____

A: Go to Gate 5 one hour before your flight.

B: _____

A: Go through Security and turn right.

When you are finished, look at your partner's paper. Is it the same as your paper?

Dialogue Exchange 122

Please say that again.
How do you spell that?

B

Dialogue Thirteen: Checking in at the Airport

Write while your partner reads. Then read while your partner writes.

A: _____

B: Here they are.

A: _____

B: This is my carry-on bag.

A: _____

B: No, I'd rather have an aisle seat, please.

A: _____

B: Where is it?

A: _____

When you are finished, look at your partner's paper. Is it the same as your paper?

Dialogue Thirteen: Checking in at the Airport

Make new sentences. Use the dialogue to help you.

1. Put your _____.

2. This is my _____.

3. Would you like _____?

4. I'd rather have _____.

5. Go to _____.

6. Where is _____?

Dialogue Thirteen: Checking in at the Airport

Vocabulary

1. flight
2. arrival
3. departure
4. baggage
5. check in
6. boarding pass
7. customs
8. seat
9. fasten
10. seatbelt
11. pillow
12. blanket
13. meal
14. toilet
15. overhead compartment
16. air sickness bag
17. headphones
18. take off
19. land
20. runway
21. flight attendant
22. pilot
23. crew
24. announcement
25. turbulence
26. life jacket
27. slide

Dialogue Thirteen: Checking in at the Airport

Discussion

1. Do you like flying? Why or why not? Does it make you nervous? Do you like window seats or aisle seats?

2. What is the best flight you have ever been on? The worst? Why?

3. Which airline do you like best? Why?

4. Should flight attendants be young and beautiful? Why or why not?

5. Would you fly first class if you had the money? Why or why not? How much does it cost? Do you collect air miles? Have you had a free trip? Where did you go?

Dialogue Fourteen: Renting a Hotel Room

Write the words for the dialogue under each picture.

Dialogue Fourteen: Renting a Hotel Room

Hello. Do you have any rooms available?
Do you want twin beds or a double bed?
How much does a double cost?
It costs $100.
That sounds okay. I'd like to see a room.
Sure, you can see room 202. Here's the key.
Thank you. I'll take it.
Can I pay for three days?
Yes, sign here and show me your passport.

Dialogue Exchange 128

Dialogue Fourteen: Renting a Hotel Room

Listen as your teacher reads. Mark the dialogue for sentence stress, intonation, linking, and reductions.

A: Hello. Do you have any rooms available?

B: Do you want twin beds or a double bed?

A: How much does a double cost?

B: It costs $100.

A: That sounds okay. I'd like to see a room.

B: Sure, you can see room 202. Here's the key.

A: Thank you. I'll take it.

A: Can I pay for three days?

B: Yes, sign here and show me your passport.

Please say that again.
How do you spell that?

A

Dialogue Fourteen: Renting a Hotel Room

Read while your partner writes. Then write while your partner reads.

A: Hello. Do you have any rooms available?

B: _____

A: How much does a double cost?

B: _____

A: That sounds okay. I'd like to see a room.

B: _____

A: Thank you. I'll take it.

A: Can I pay for three days?

B: _____

When you are finished, look at your partner's paper. Is it the same as your paper?

Please say that again.
How do you spell that?

B

Dialogue Fourteen: Renting a Hotel Room

Read while your partner writes. Then write while your partner reads.

A: _____

B: Do you want twin beds or a double bed?

A: _____

B: It costs $100.

A: _____

B: Sure, you can see room 202. Here's the key.

A: _____

A: _____

B: Yes, sign here and show me your passport.

When you are finished, look at your partner's paper. Is it the same as your paper?

Dialogue Fourteen: Renting a Hotel Room

Make new sentences. Use the dialogue to help you.

1. Do you want _____?

2. How much does _____?

3. It costs _____.

4. That sounds _____.

5. Can I pay _____?

6. Show me _____.

Dialogue Exchange

Dialogue Fourteen: Renting a Hotel Room

Vocabulary

1. motel
2. hostel
3. guesthouse
4. bed and breakfast (B and B)
5. homestay
6. reservation
7. (no) vacancy
8. front desk
9. check in
10. check out
11. tour
12. shuttle
13. wake-up call
14. safe
15. valuables
16. laundry
17. sheet
18. towel
19. blanket
20. soap
21. shampoo
22. housekeeping
23. noise
24. clean
25. (doesn't) work
26. locked out
27. Who is it?

Dialogue Fourteen: Renting a Hotel Room

Discussion

1. What was the best vacation you have ever been on? Why? What was the worst vacation you have ever been on? Why?

2. Have you ever booked a hotel room online? Which websites do you use? Do you like them?

3. What is your favourite hotel? Have you stayed there? Have you eaten in the restaurant?

4. Where would you like to go on your next trip? Where would you go if you won a free trip anywhere in the world?

5. What does a good hotel have? Name five things.

Dialogue Fifteen: Taking a Taxi

Write the words for the dialogue under each picture.

Dialogue Exchange 135

Dialogue Fifteen: Taking a Taxi

Taxi!
Can you take me to 3602 Broadway?
Do you want East or West Broadway?
The address is 3602 West Broadway.
What's the cross street?
It's Alma Street. It's near the university.
Oh, okay. I know where that is. Get in.
How far is it from here?
It's about 15 minutes drive.

Dialogue Fifteen: Taking a Taxi

Listen as your teacher reads. Mark the dialogue for sentence stress, intonation, linking, and reductions.

A: Taxi!

A: Can you take me to 3602 Broadway?

B: Do you want East or West Broadway?

A: The address is 3602 West Broadway.

B: What's the cross street?

A: It's Alma Street. It's near the university.

B: Oh, okay. I know where that is. Get in.

A: How far is it from here?

B: It's about 15 minutes away.

Please say that again.
How do you spell that?

A

Dialogue Fifteen: Taking a Taxi

Read while your partner writes. Then write while your partner reads.

A: Taxi!

A: Can you take me to 3602 Broadway?

B: _____

A: The address is 3602 West Broadway.

B: _____

A: It's Alma Street. It's near the university.

B: _____

A: How far is it from here?

B: _____

When you are finished, look at your partner's paper. Is it the same as your paper?

Please say that again.
How do you spell that?

B

Dialogue Fifteen: Taking a Taxi

Write while your partner reads. Then read while your partner writes.

A: _____

A: _____

B: Do you want East or West Broadway?

A: _____

B: What's the cross street?

A: _____

B: Oh, okay. I know where that is. Get in.

A: _____

B: It's about 15 minutes away.

When you are finished, look at your partner's paper. Is it the same as your paper?

Dialogue Fifteen: Taking a Taxi

Make new sentences. Use the dialogue to help you.

1. Can you take me to_____?

2. Do you want_____?

3. What's the_____?

4. It's near_____.

5. I know where_____.

6. How far is_____?

Dialogue Exchange 140

Dialogue Fifteen: Taking a Taxi

Vocabulary

1. meter
2. fare
3. taxi stand
4. radio
5. flag
6. front seat
7. back seat
8. drive
9. stop
10. go straight
11. turn right/left
12. slow down
13. wait
14. pull over
15. park
16. pick me up
17. drop me off
18. take me (back) to
19. let me out
20. give directions
21. get lost
22. gas
23. brake
24. trunk
25. turn signal
26. headlights
27. How much does it cost to go to _____?

Dialogue Fifteen: Taking a Taxi

Discussion

1. Are taxi fares expensive here? Would you rather take transit? Why or why not?

2. Do you feel safe in taxis? Why or why not? What can you do to feel safer?

3. How are taxis different in different parts of the world? Do you talk to taxi drivers? Do you sit in the front seat or the back seat? Why?

4. How do you feel if the driver doesn't want to use the meter? What do you do?

5. Do you think driving a taxi would be a good job? Why or why not? Do you think taxi drivers make good money? Do you tip taxi drivers? How much?

Appendices and Grids

Dialogue Exchange 144

Appendix A
Teaching the Basics

First Day

Have all the students stand in a circle. Throw a **stuffed animal** to one of the students and ask, "What is your name?" The student answers, and then throws the stuffed animal to another student. Continue until everyone has had a turn. Repeat with, "Where are you from?", and "What are you doing in _____?"

Countries

This is a good activity for the first day of class. Give each student **a sticky label and a pin**. Have each student write his or her name on the label and wrap it around the pin. Put the pins in a **wall map**. Pair up the students. Have each student say, "(Partner's name) is from _____."

Write the names of your students' countries on the board and add a few more to equal about 20. Read and have the class repeat after you. When you are finished, have students copy in their notebooks.

You may also want to teach the adjectives, plus pronouns, and the verb "to be". For example:

    I am Canadian.   We are Russian.
    You are Korean.   You are Polish.
    He is Japanese.   They are Guatemalan.

Review

Review countries using Password, Sticky Note Mingle, or the Drawing Game (pages 15 and 17).

Food

Collages

Bring **food magazines and supermarket junk mail** to class and have students make collages. You will also need **large sheets of paper, glue sticks, several pairs of scissors, tape or tacks, and a felt pen.** Write the names of the food items on the collages. (Start labeling the collages as soon as the students start making them. Otherwise, students may not see the point of the activity.) When the collages are finished, pin them on the wall. Walk the students around the classroom. Read and have the class repeat the vocabulary after you. Next, have students write sentences, such as:

I (don't) like _____.
_____ is (not) good for you.
_____ is delicious.
I eat _____ every day.
I am eating _____ now.

Leave the collages on the wall so students can study them when they have a few minutes before class. Collages can also be used to teach shopping or renting an apartment.

Review

Review the material using the Drawing Game (page 17). Teach some adjectives, and play Vocabulary Pick-Up Cards, the Vocabulary Board Game, Password, or Sticky Note Mingle (pages 14 and 15).

Field Trip

Take students on a field trip to a grocery store or farmers' market. When you are at the market, put students in pairs and give them a scavengers' hunt **worksheet**. For example:

> 1. Find five yellow vegetables.
> 2. How much do chicken wings cost?
> 3. What is the cheapest fruit?
> 4. What is the most expensive cheese?
> 5. ....

Elicit or provide explanations for vocabulary, then pair up students and give them free time to find the answers. Go through the answers when you return to class.

The next day, elicit a Language Experience Approach narrative about the field trip from the students. Write the narrative on the board as the students dictate, expanding and developing where necessary. For example:

> Yesterday we went to Granville Island. It was sunny and warm. We took the bus to Fourth Avenue, and then we walked under the bridges. First we went to the market. There were many people selling food...........

When you have finished writing, read the first phrase of the narrative as you run your hand below the words, then have the students repeat as a class. Continue this way until you have read the whole narrative, and then have each student read a sentence individually. This exercise will help students connect written and spoken language, and will help them develop reading skills in English, so they can learn without the teacher being present.

The narrative can be used to focus on a particular aspect of English, such as the past tense or sentence stress. For example, ask students to identify the past tense verbs, and then have them provide the present tense form.

When you are finished, have the students copy the narrative into their notebooks. On a subsequent day, write questions for the statements in the narrative and have students answer them or make a pair dictation.

For example:

A

Yesterday we went to Granville Island. _____ . We took the

bus to Fourth Avenue, _____. First we went to the market.

_____..............

B

_____. It was sunny and warm. _____,

and then we walked under the bridges. _____.

There were many people selling food..................

Have students read to each other and then compare papers when they are finished.

Cooking Class

If you have the facilities, make a dish with your class. When you are finished cooking, elicit the recipe from the students. Write it on the board as students dictate, expanding and developing where necessary. Read and have the class repeat after you, then have the class copy. Recipes can be used to focus on the imperative tense. Make a cloze exercise or a pair dictation from the recipe for use on a subsequent date.

Vietnamese salad rolls work very well for this activity, because they are cheap, they can be made with a **kettle**, **a couple of bowls**, and **some clean tea towels**, and each student can make his or her own.

Numbers

Write on the board the Arabic numerals up to ten. Elicit their names and write these on the board. Read and have students repeat. Have students copy. Practice numbers at random with **flash cards**, then have students repeat this activity in groups. Add more numbers.

Go Fish

You will need a **deck of playing cards for each group**. This game also gives students practice with "Do you have a(n)....?" plus short answers. Write these on the board before you begin. Model the game with three higher students. Deal five cards to each player and put the rest of the cards in a pile on the table, face down. The first player asks any of the others for a card that matches a card in the first player's hand. If the second player has it, he gives the card to the first player who puts the pair on the table and takes another turn. If the second player doesn't have it, the first player takes a card from the pile and his turn ends. When a player runs out of cards, he draws two more from the pile. The person with the most pairs in the end wins. If you wish, you can use the face cards as 11, 12, and 13.

99

This card game is a fun way to practice numbers up to 99. Write on the board of all the Arabic numerals between one and 30, as well as 40, 50, 60, 70, 80, and 90. Elicit the names of the numbers and write them on the board. Read and have students repeat after you. Let students copy when you have finished speaking.

You will need a **deck of playing cards for each group of four students**. Each player begins the game with four **gummy bears (or pennies)**. Model the game with some of the higher students.

Deal five cards to each player. Place the remaining cards face down on the table. The player to the left of the dealer starts, and then each player takes a turn in a clockwise direction. The first player lays down a card face up, calls out the value of that card, and then takes another card from the pile. The second player lays down a card, calls out the total value of both cards, and takes another card from the pile. The third player lays down a card and calls out the value of all three cards, and so on. The following cards have special powers:

10	minus ten
Jack	miss a turn
Queen	change direction
King	99

Players must avoid going over 99. If a player can't, that round ends, and one of the other players eats one of the losing player's gummy bears. They keep playing until only one player still has gummy bears. That player wins.

Some groups of students may not like the scorekeeping aspect of this game. If this is the case, the game can be modified: Don't use pennies or gummy bears. Just play several rounds and don't keep score. This game can be played two or three times on subsequent days or until the students get adequate practice with numbers.

Larger Numbers

Write some larger numbers on the board. Elicit the English and write it on the board. Read the words and have students repeat as a class. When you are finished, have students copy the words. Do several examples. Make a pair dictation to practice larger numbers. Repeat for phone numbers, postal codes, and so on. Play Vocabulary Pick Up Cards (page 14).

Parts of the Body

Draw a picture of a person on the board. Elicit the names of the body parts from the class and label the drawing. When you are finished, have the class copy from the board. Read and have students repeat as a class.

Simon Says Please

Instead of using "Simon," use "please," "can you please," or "could you please." Stand in front of the class and have students stand as well. If you say, "Please put your hands on your hips," or "Can you please touch your ear," students do it. If you don't say "please," then students do nothing. If a student does it anyway, then that student has to sit down. The last student standing wins the game. Repeat with a student acting as the leader.

Review

Play the Drawing Game (page 17). Have students reproduce the various body parts on the board. Award an extra point if the team can use the word in a sentence: "I have a sore _____," or "My _____ hurts."

Dates

Draw a calendar page on the board. Elicit the days of the week from the students, write them on the board, and have students copy. Read and have students repeat as a class.

Write the numbers 1 to 12 on the board. Elicit the names of the months from the students, write them on the board. Read and have students repeat as a class. Have students copy when you are finished.

Ensure that students can say the year correctly, and that they know the seasons.

Review

Review dates using Blanks on the Board or Dictation Relay (pages 17 and 18), or make a Pair Dictation.

Time

Draw a clock on the board and write on the left side "to" and on the right side "after" and "past." Have students copy. Draw hands on the clock and ask students the time. Use several examples, and have students answer individually, giving easier tasks to lower students.

Review

Make a Pair Dictation or have a Dictation Relay (page 18). Play Vocabulary Pick-Up Cards (page 14). Write digital time on cards, but call out more difficult examples and have students match them.

Divide the class into two or more teams and have one person from each team come to the board. Call out "twenty to twelve" and so on, and have students write the digital time on the board. Award a point to the team that gets the correct answer first. Make sure everyone gets a turn at the board. The team with the most points wins.

Appendix B
Reference Material for Pronunciation

These items can be introduced to students through choral repetition or through listening exercises (see pages 5, 6 and 8). Although traditionally rhythm is not always taught to beginners, we do expect them to learn punctuation, capitalization, and a spelling system that defies logic. Like writing, speech has rules that can be taught, and leaving them too late can lead to fossilized errors at higher levels. A little bit of structure can go a long way.

Sentence Stress

Sentence stress falls on the stressed syllable of the most important content word in a sentence. These words will normally be nouns, verbs, adjectives, adverbs, question words, and negative contractions. Stressed vowels will be longer, louder, clearer, and higher.

Most sentences will have only one or sometimes two words that have the highest level of sentence stress. Function words, such as "of" and "the" have the lowest level stress, while some words in the sentence have a medium level of stress.

I recommend drawing attention to the highest level of sentence stress, so students' speech develops a more natural English rhythm, and they are easier to understand. If the students' first language is syllable-timed, rather than stress-timed, their speech in English may sound staccato or monotone. Listening for sentence stress should be fairly easy for students.

Intonation

Intonation refers to the pitch of the speaker's voice. In English, a rising pitch is used

- for yes or no questions
- for items on a list, with the exception of the last item
- for a polite request (rather than a command)
- as a part of sentence stress in order to signal important information (see above)

Most other utterances, including information questions, normally end with a falling pitch. Students, especially those whose first language has tones, will sometimes have too many rising pitches. This communicates uncertainty and can make them sound unsure of themselves when they speak English. Also, the listener may think that the speaker is not finished even though he is. Intonation has a few other uses, such as separating thought groups, but these can be saved for intermediate classes.

Linking

Linking occurs in English when two or more words are spoken together so quickly that they sound like one word. The timing is the same. For example, "euthanasia" and "youth in Asia" are identical when spoken. Linking relies on sound rather than spelling.

Linking is more challenging for students. It can be introduced at an upper beginner level, starting with consonant-to-vowel linking, with more sophisticated forms left for later classes. Technical explanations should be kept brief. Linking makes listening difficult for students, and mastering it will greatly improve their skills, but too much emphasis on this material at beginner levels is usually not a good idea.

Here are the basic rules for linking in English:

- Consonants link to following vowels. For example:

    can‿I
    name‿is
    watch‿out!

- Similar or identical consonants, with the exception of affricates, link to each other. For example:

    from‿Mexico
    have‿fun
    feels‿sick

- Affricates, [j] and [ch], don't link to each other. For example:

    orange juice
    each child

- Tense vowels link to following vowels. This type of linking is more difficult and can be saved for later classes. Four tense vowels end in a [y] semi-vowel, and this sound links to any following vowel. For example:

    h**e**‿is   [iy]
    th**ey**‿are   [ey]
    I‿am   [aɪ]
    b**oy**‿is   [ɔɪ]

- The remaining three tense vowels end in a [w] semi-vowel, and this sound links to any following vowel. For example:

    n**o**⌣answer   [ow]
    wh**o**⌣is   [uw]
    h**ow**⌣are   [aʊ]

The remaining vowels are lax and do not have semi-vowel endings, so they do not link to the following vowel. Linking involves a few other complications, but these should be saved for intermediate level.

Reductions

Reductions are words and phrases that have the lowest level of stress. Function words, such as articles, prepositions, pronouns, auxiliary verbs, the verb "to be," and affirmative contractions are commonly reduced, because they contain less information than stressed words. Reductions are more difficult for students to identify than sentence stress, as reduced words are often difficult for them to hear. Reduced words will often go missing in students' speech.

The most common reduction is the schwa or unstressed vowel. One third of all English vowels are reduced to schwa, and schwa can be spelled a, e, i, o, or u. I recommend introducing the schwa to higher beginners who have a good level of education. It shouldn't be taught in depth at this level. Technical explanations should be brief or avoided altogether.

Function words are frequently reduced to schwa. For example, in the sentence, "I'd like a table for two," both "a" and "for" have unstressed vowels, or schwas. If they are given the same level of stress as "table" or "two," the speaker sounds angry, not a good thing when making a polite request. That's why reductions are an important aspect of English.

Another common reduction is the contraction. Native speakers use contractions about 90 per cent of the time. Speakers who don't use contractions sound angry and may give their listeners the wrong impression. Some contractions are not commonly written, but are often present in speech. For example, "What are you doing?" is usually pronounced, "What're you doing?" but it is not usually written that way. When there's no contraction, the question can sound demanding. If you draw students' attention to contractions, both written and unwritten, their English will sound more natural, their listening and speaking skills will improve, and they will have better experiences with native speakers.

In North American English, the [t] is usually reduced to something that sounds similar to a [d] when it is between two vowels, as in "better." Students who are taught basic linguistic rules will sound more natural and have less trouble understanding native speakers. Reductions vary from one English dialect to another.

Frequently Asked Questions

Is this book for students or teachers?
It is intended as a teaching manual. Although students may get something from the book if they study by themselves, a teacher, or at least a fluent language partner, is required to provide material in some sections, such as New and Related Dialogues.

Are these materials best-suited for immigrants and refugees, international students, or for English as a foreign language?
Almost all of the activities can be used with any group; however, international and EFL students generally respond better to a faster, more difficult pace. With immigrants and refugees, a slower pace, at least for the first few days, might be a better choice.

On the first day of class, aim a bit high if you have international or EFL students and a bit low if you have immigrants and refugees. You can adjust the pace as you get used to the level of the class.

As well, you may want to omit some chapters if they don't suit the needs of your class. For example, if you are teaching refugees, you may want to omit chapters on hotel rooms and taxis. These chapters can be taught much earlier than they appear in the book if you are teaching visitors or teaching English as a foreign language.

Once you have taught chapters that you or your school consider most important, you can let the class choose additional chapters. Photocopy the Contents page, hand it out to students, and let them vote on which chapters they would like to study. Students appreciate choice.

Why isn't some of the material that I want to teach included in your book?
You can incorporate this material yourself under the New and Related Dialogue section or add it to the Vocabulary Lists. Use the various activities to review it.

It is sometimes a good idea to ask students a few days before the course ends if there is any other material that they would like to study or review. Doing this will give you a chance to meet their needs, and it will encourage students to take some responsibility for what they learn.

What can I do to improve attendance?
Learn students' names right away and use them often. Enforce the attendance policy at your school. Let students know in a friendly way that you notice when they are away. Start the class on time every day, and cultivate a professional, business-like manner and appearance.

Make the class a pleasant, social place where the students want to be. Make sure each student works with every one of his peers. Encourage friendships between students, especially cross-cultural ones.

Organize the physical classroom to best suit your situation. Desks in U shapes work well.

My students' eyes are glazing over. What should I do?
Limit teacher talk. Elicit rather than provide information as much as possible. Speak at about 50 per cent of normal speed, using natural rhythm. Exaggerate pauses between sentences, and use hand signals. Edit out difficult vocabulary, complex grammatical structures, and needless information. Use the imperative tense to summarize: "I talk, you write." Speaking this way takes practice, but soon you'll find yourself doing it to your friends!

Check for comprehension regularly. Don't ask students, "Do you understand?" They will almost always say yes. Instead, ask information questions that require students to prove that they understand. Have students write "I understand _____% when the teacher is talking" on a piece of paper and give the papers to you anonymously. If they don't understand what you're saying, keep trying. See above. Check again in a month and see if percentages improve.

End or change activities before students get bored, usually after about 20 to 30 minutes.

Ensure that students have been properly assessed.

Some of my students don't want to work with each other.
Insist. For some activities, it is best to give groups one worksheet to share, then hand out additional copies when the activity is over.

Some of my students don't like games.
Some students, particularly those with traditional educational backgrounds, may initially resist playing games. This usually won't persist if they can see a clear purpose to the activity and if the activities are balanced with more traditional, written work such as dictations and dialogues. With some classes, it may be advisable to call what you are doing an activity rather than a game. Keep games short—it's better to leave students wanting more than to bore them. Shifting activities from the beginning to the end of the lesson and vice versa can sometimes yield dramatic results. Relatively light activities such as games often work best at the beginning of class, particularly if it is a morning class, and the students are half-awake.

My students speak very quietly, especially when they are speaking in front of the class. How can I help them be more confident?
Provide positive feedback throughout the lesson. Make sure you are standing as far away from them as possible, so that they project their voices. If they continue to speak too quietly, have them repeat what they are saying. Don't repeat it for them.

Why is there a chapter on applying for a job? Isn't this too much for beginners?
Some students need to find a job soon after they arrive in a new country, because they need to support themselves or their families. These individuals can sometimes feel frustrated and anxious if this reality is not addressed. While your students may not be interview-ready after you teach the lesson, some will appreciate progress in that direction.

Blank Grid

Dialogue Exchange 156

Card Grid

Dialogue Exchange 157

Board Game

Start	1	2	3
4	5	6	7
8	9	10	11
12	13	14	15
16	17	18	19
20	21	22	Finish

Dialogue Exchange 158